22.60

W9-CIH-373

A Beginning-to-Read Book

EARTH SCIENCE

SUN AND SHADE

by Mary Lindeen

NORWOOD HOUSE PRESS

DEAR CAREGIVER, The *Beginning to Read—Read and Discover Science* books provide young readers the opportunity to learn about scientific concepts while simultaneously building early reading skills. Each title corresponds to three of the key domains within the Next Generation Science Standards (NGSS): physical sciences, life sciences, and earth and space sciences.

The NGSS include standards that are comprised of three dimensions: Cross-cutting Concepts, Science and Engineering Practices, and Disciplinary Core Ideas. The texts within the *Read and Discover Science* series focus primarily upon the Disciplinary Core Ideas and Cross-cutting Concepts—helping readers view their world through a scientific lens. They pique a young reader's curiosity and encourage them to inquire and explore. The Connecting Concepts section at the back of each book offers resources to continue that exploration. The reinforcement activities at the back of the book support Science and Engineering Practices—to understand how scientists investigate phenomena in that world.

These easy-to-read informational texts make the scientific concepts accessible to young readers and prompt them to consider the role of science in their world. On one hand, these titles can develop background knowledge for exploring new topics. Alternately, they can be used to investigate, explain, and expand the findings of one's own inquiry. As you read with your child, encourage her or him to "observe"—taking notice of the images and information to formulate both questions and responses about what, how, and why something is happening.

Above all, the most important part of the reading experience is to have fun and enjoy it!

Sincerely,

Shannon Cannon

Shannon Cannon, Ph.D.
Literacy Consultant

Norwood House Press • P.O. Box 316598 • Chicago, Illinois 60631
For more information about Norwood House Press please visit our website at
www.norwoodhousepress.com or call 866-565-2900.
© 2018 Norwood House Press. Beginning-to-Read™ is a trademark of Norwood House Press.
All rights reserved. No part of this book may be reproduced or utilized in any form or by any
means without written permission from the publisher.

Editor: Judy Kentor Schmauss
Designer: Lindaanne Donohoe

Photo Credits:
All photos by Shutterstock except: NASA/SDO, 6-7

Library of Congress Cataloging-in-Publication Data
    Names: Lindeen, Mary, author.
    Title: Sun and shade / by Mary Lindeen.
    Description: Chicago, IL : Norwood House Press, [2017] | Series: A beginning
       to read book | Audience: K to grade 3.
    Identifiers: LCCN 2017002627 (print) | LCCN 2017021603 (ebook) | ISBN
       9781684041046 (eBook) | ISBN 9781599538723 (library edition : alk. paper)
    Subjects: LCSH: Temperature-Juvenile literature. | Heat-Juvenile
       literature. | Sun-Juvenile literature.
    Classification: LCC QC271.4 (ebook) | LCC QC271.4 .L56 2017 (print) | DDC
       536–dc23
    LC record available at https://lccn.loc.gov/2017002627

    Library ISBN: 978-1-59953-872-3   Paperback ISBN: 978-1-68404-091-9

302N—072017
Manufactured in the United States of America in North Mankato, Minnesota.

These sunflowers look like the sun.
And they need the sun to stay alive.
So do you!

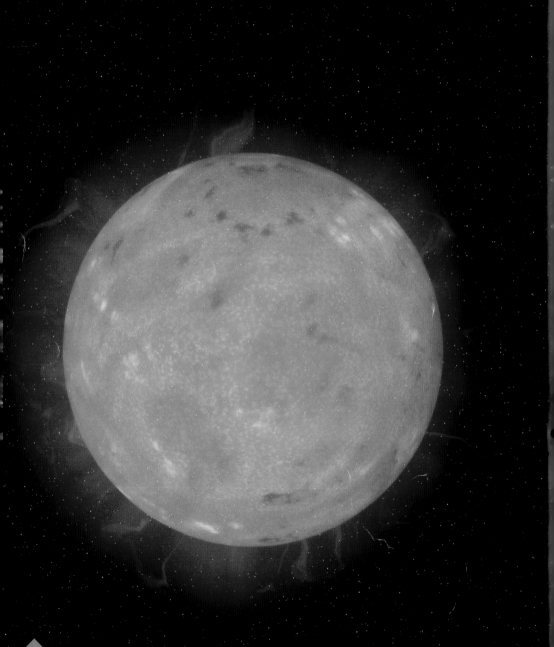

The sun is a star.

It's closer to Earth than
any other star.

Stars are made of hot burning gases.

So the sun is really a big ball of fire.

That's why it gives off so much heat and light.

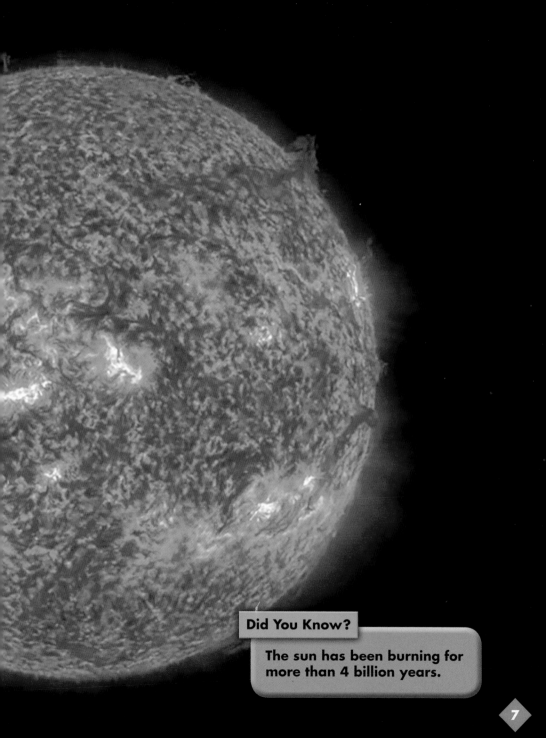

Did You Know?

The sun has been burning for more than 4 billion years.

People, plants, and animals need the sun's heat to keep them warm.

They need the sun's light to help grow their food.

Did You Know?

Sunscreen can protect your skin from getting burned by the sun.

Sometimes the sun feels
too hot and bright.

People who get
too much sun
can get a
sunburn.

But plants that get too much
sun can dry up and die.

Sometimes it's helpful to block some of the sun's light.

Blocked sunlight makes a shadow called shade.

Shade can come from nature.

This big tree makes
a lot of shade.

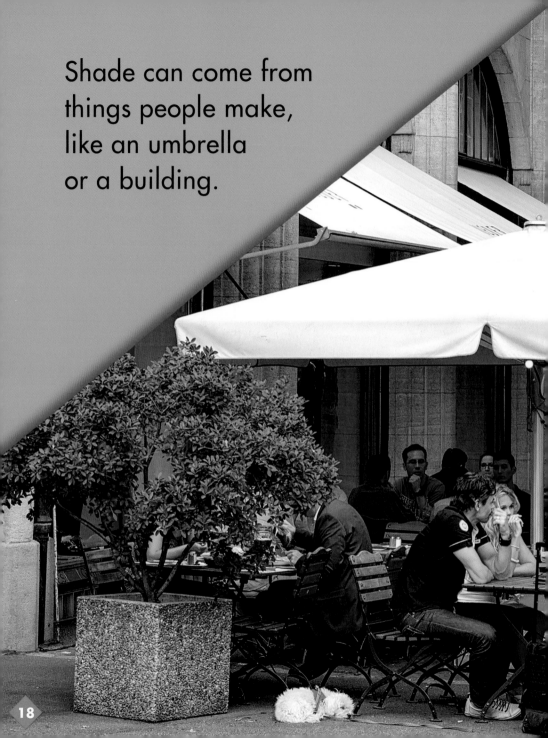

Shade can come from
things people make,
like an umbrella
or a building.

Some plants can only grow
in bright sunlight.

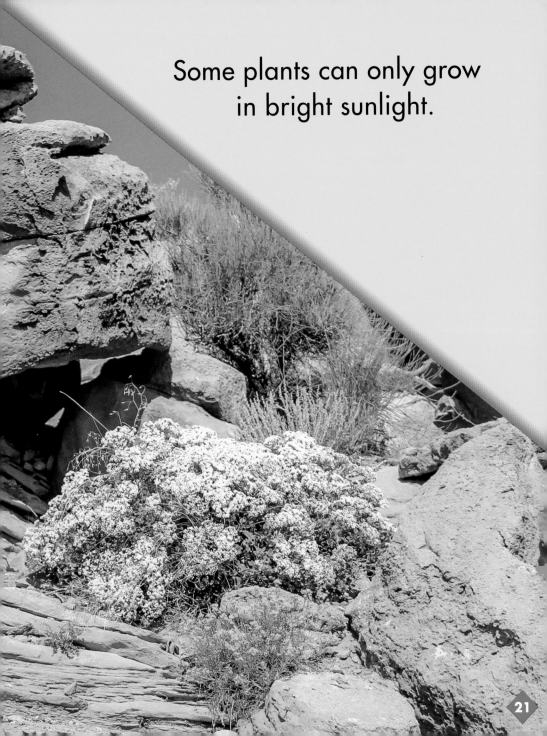

But some plants can only grow in the shade.

Sometimes people like to be
in the sun.

It's warmer there.

But sometimes people like
to be in the shade.

It's cooler there.

What about you?
Do you like the sun or the shade better?

Sun

Shade

CONNECTING CONCEPTS

CLOSE READING OF NONFICTION TEXT

Close reading helps children comprehend text. It includes reading a text, discussing it with others, and answering questions about it. Use these questions to discuss this book with your child:

- What is the sun made out of?
- Explain why the sun gives off so much heat and light.
- What would happen to plants if the sun stopped shining? What would happen to animals?
- Why might it be very hot in a desert area that does not have a lot of trees?
- Why might it stay cool in a forest where there are lots of trees?
- How would you know if a plant was getting too much sun?

SCIENCE IN THE REAL WORLD

Have your child divide a piece of construction paper in half. Cover the palm of his or her hand with sunscreen. Press it down on one side of the paper. Put the paper in the sun for several hours. Talk about why the handprint stayed the same color but the rest of the paper faded from the sun's heat and light.

SCIENCE AND ACADEMIC LANGUAGE

Make sure your child understands the meaning of the following words:

alive	star	gases	heat	light	sunburn
protect	die	block	shadow	shade	

Have him or her use the words in a sentence.

FLUENCY

Fluency is the ability to read accurately with speed and expression.
Help your child practice fluency by using one or more of the following activities:

1. Reread the book to your child at least two times while he or she uses a finger to track each word as it is read.

2. Read a line of the book, then reread it as your child reads along with you.

3. Ask your child to go back through the book and read the words he or she knows.

4. Have your child practice reading the book several times to improve accuracy, rate, and expression.

FOR FURTHER INFORMATION

Books:

DeCristofano, Carolyn Cinami. *The Sun and the Moon*. New York, NY: HarperCollins, 2016.

Demuth, Patricia B. *The Sun: Our Amazing Star*. New York, NY: Grosset and Dunlap, 2016.

Taylor-Butler, Christine. *The Sun*. New York, NY: Children's Press, 2014.

Websites:

Kids Health: How to Be Safe When You're in the Sun

http://kidshealth.org/en/kids/summer-safety.html?ref=search#

Meet Sunwise Animals

https://www.foundation.sdsu.edu/sunwisestampede/meetanimals.html

Space Facts for Kids: The Sun Facts and Information

http://space-kids.org/the-sun/

Sun and Shade uses the 102 words listed below. *High-frequency* words are those words that are used most often in the English language. They are sometimes referred to as sight words because children need to learn to recognize them automatically when they read. *Content words* are any words specific to a particular topic. Regular practice reading these words will enhance your child's ability to read with greater fluency and comprehension.

High-Frequency Words

a	but	give(s)	make(s)	so	they	years
about	by	has	more	some	things	you
an	called	help(ful)	much	than	this	your
and	can	in	of	that	to	
any	come	is	off	the	too	
are	do	it	only	their	up	
be	for	like	or	them	what	
been	from	look	other	there	who	
big	get(ing)	made	people	these	why	

Content Words

alive	building	Earth	hot	plants	star(s)	that's
animals	burn(ed,	feels	it's	protect	stay	tree
ball	ing)	fire	keep	really	sun('s)	umbrella
better	closer	food	light	shade	sunburn	warm(er)
billion	cooler	gases	lot	shadow	sunscreen	
block(ed)	die	grow	nature	skin	sunflowers	
bright	dry	heat	need	sometimes	sunlight	

About the Author

Mary Lindeen is a writer, editor, parent, and former elementary school teacher. She has written more than 100 books for children and edited many more. She specializes in early literacy instruction and books for young readers, especially nonfiction.

About the Advisor

Dr. Shannon Cannon is an elementary school teacher in Sacramento, California. She has served as a teacher educator in the School of Education at UC Davis, where she also earned her Ph.D. in Language, Literacy, and Culture. As a member of the clinical faculty, she supervised pre-service teachers and taught elementary methods courses in reading, effective teaching, and teacher action research.